The 3

Day

Servant

Leader

Dr. Dustin D. Hofheins

Dedication

To my associates.

CONTENTS

About the Author

My name is Dustin D. Hofheins, and I have been a job coach for a nonprofit organization for the last eight years. I am married to an amazingly gorgeous and beautiful English woman, and we have four amazing children together: two boys and two girls. I tripped over the finish line of a bachelor's degree in business administration, stumbled over the finish line for a master's degree in business administration, and passed out and accidentally fell over the finish line for doctorate degree in business administration. I spent 11 years studying, observing, and researching the topic of servant leadership while completing my doctorate (I would not suggest this!!... it was horrifyingly hard!!).

Cover Picture Title:

The Servant Leader About Doing Good

Introduction

Hopefully, this book is going to be fun and very unacademic in nature, with a new nonchalant and sarcastic writing style. I wrote a dissertation on servant leadership that took me eight years to finish and everything I said had to be backed up with research. It was like I was stuck in a box for eight years and was only allowed to write a certain way. I think if I start citing research, I might start intermittently crying, shaking, and curling up in a ball from the excruciating memories of writing my dissertation.

This is going to be an easy-going servant leadership book. While the principles I suggest can be backed up with academic research, I am just going to be real about what I have observed and learned about being the most amazing servant leader on this bright blue earth!! Patterned after Jesus Christ of course!!! This book is titled *The 3 Day Servant Leader* for a couple of reasons. First, I am endeavoring to write and publish this book in a three-day period. I just want to see if I can do it! This is crazy! I already know! That is why I am doing it! Second, I am going to organize it in a way that can be read and presented in three separate leadership training sessions.

I seem to be made up a little different than others. If you have ever read *The Color Code by Taylor Hartman*... I am a dominant yellow and a secondary blue personality. This essentially means that I can be fun, the life of the party, spontaneous, sometimes irresponsible as a yellow can be, but also feel deep feelings, and seem to be keenly aware of how others are feeling. I can be fun and irresponsible, but I have consciousness that quickly throws me back on track before I deviate too far. It's a vicious cycle...lol.

I have always loved doing things that seem to be impossible, or that a normal person would not consider doing. Like when I attempted to run a marathon with zero days of training... That was a disaster by the way!... but makes for a hilarious and amazing story. I usually end up falling flat on my face during my attempts at the impossible but that makes the journey even more interesting. My doctorate was supposed to take only three years after getting an MBA... It took me 11! Yes, 11 years of pure unadulterated doctoral heckness! Yes, I invent words as well! But you know, if I could go back, I would not do anything different. The hardest, most desperate times of my life are what have made me, and I hope that you are one of the beneficiaries of my ups and downs of learning and practicing the most amazing leadership theory on Earth SERVANT LEADERSHIP!

I have found that it is important to always be working on a Big Harry Audacious Goal that scares you to death! Anyway, thank you for reading *The 3 Day Servant Leader!* I am super passionate about the subject! I hope it changes everything for you and makes all your wildest dreams come true! As long as your wildest dreams include being more like Jesus in your leadership style, I have got you covered!! Sprinkled with a few laughs of course!

Chapter One

My Leadership Journey

Every leader has a leadership journey, so I am going to start by telling you mine. It is really exciting, so this might be the time to drink your caffeinated drink of choice! Might I suggest Diet Mt. Dew! The pure nectar of the vine!

It all started in the year of 2008 and 2009. I

was just about to graduate with the coveted MBA degree. I had spent every moment of my spare time studying investments and had just passed the Series 7 stockbroker exam. I was ready! I was going to be the next millionaire investment guru... heck, why stop at millionaire? I was going to be the next billionaire! All my education had led me to this moment. Sure, the great recession of 2008 was rearing its ugly head, the Dow Jones Industrial Average had just dipped to around 6,500, and most investment firms were shedding employees... but was I going to let the largest global recession since the Great Depression stop my dreams? No way! I had a flipping MBA! You can't stop someone armed with an MBA! MBA's don't fail! Let's do the impossible!

One of my great friends from high school and I found a firm that was hiring for commission only positions and we literally threw everything we had at it. We worked 6 days per week (morning till night), knocked doors, cold called, joined networking clubs, ate lunch with teachers, took clients to dinner, conducted seminars, walked in parades, "held and kissed babies,"... I think you get my point! We also brought in as many accounts from family members as we could and scared away our remaining friends and family. After two and a half years of milking every resource to make it in the financial industry...well...we didn't...I didn't. And when I say I didn't make it, I mean I went bankrupt. I lost everything that was not important!

Having couriers waiting at your house to deliver court documents for unpaid bills is a scrumptiously tantalizing experience that I would definitely recommend! I mean... you have not lived until you have experienced this type of economic action! And do you know what happens when your credit score takes a bankruptcy ding when working in the financial industry? You are barred from working in the financial industry. Which was great! All I could think was.... Yes!! This is what winning feels like!!!   Yes!!! It's not like I put all my educational eggs in this basket or anything!

All laughing aside... I loved investments more than anything else I had studied, and spending a couple of years working with one of my best friends was a dream of epic proportions. We would spend most of the day laughing while we experienced heaps of rejection with the occasional small win along the way.   At the time I had just finished my first professional designation as an Accredited Asset Management Specialist AAMS (I am glad I did that if you know what I mean).

Is this a good time to mention that I also get sick and want to curl up in a ball when I see a finance book of any kind!   I donated all my school investment textbooks and my whole investment library to a local thrift store... It was better than burning them... which is what I wanted to do! I then decided that it was time to reinvent myself by beginning a doctorate degree and washing my hands of finance. I was also now going to find a job working for "the man" or "the woman" (you must be all inclusive these days). I don't want to get in trouble. There are plenty of bad woman managers as well!

See I grew up working for my dad's masonry company, I ran my own masonry repair business, and ran our own property management company. I had, for the most part, experienced a lot of autonomy and respect at every job up until this point. I was in control of my destiny. Even my finance job, if you can call it that... Do you have to make money at a job to call it a job? huh... maybe it wasn't a real job... Anyway... making money or not, I had autonomy and respect from others in finance.

This was a situation that I had never found myself in. The invisible hand of the investment market economy had beat me down to a level I had not experienced. I had experienced a lack of financial inflows that had brought our family to its economic knees. Too many famines, and not enough feasts if you know what I mean!

Now, if you ever want to feel like a real man this is the situation you want to be in! Raw feelings of manliness! I actually think the hairs on my chest were receding and sucking themselves back into my body. It was like my chest was saying "You don't deserve this hair anymore! We will start growing again when you start providing for your family!" So, I started rubbing Rogaine on my chest in manliness desperation!!! HaHaHa!

I landed some jobs after this point... all sales jobs... but that is beside the point. For the next handful or so of years I ended up selling multiple types of products for multiple types of organizations, but without the autonomy or respect that I was used to when working for myself or my family. Speaking of chest hair... if you want to grow it and become a real man sales jobs are the way to go! It takes a real man or real woman to sell! It makes or breaks you... this is for sure!

As I was working for these various sales organizations, I found myself curious and in shock at what I was experiencing while working for "the man." It was like I was placed with some of the best managers on earth, and some of the worst managers on earth, and the contrast in leadership styles and their effects on the employees' happiness, performance, and retention was astounding!

I am the first to admit that I did not respond very well to some of the situations that I found myself in. I would suggest now... with perfect vision hindsight... that it is better to build bridges than to tear them down, light them on fire, and give them the California howdy on the way out!

Honestly, some of my greatest growing pains have come from these amazing experiences where I did not make the right decision. There are some bridges that I burnt that I don't know if any amount of repair will be fixed. Jesus is my only hope for those relationships! It seems like we all need to go through these mistakes before we learn the importance of kindness and civility. I have a couple of stories and quotes about kindness that we will go over later in the book but let's just say that I have learned from sad experience, that one wrong cannot be corrected with another wrong. It is better to turn the other check as Jesus councils I don't know how he did it, but the few times I have been able to do it, let's just say the outcome was much better.

Ok, back to the story...so I started to notice that the leadership style of my various managers had a tremendous effect on employee happiness and employee performance at work. Some managers knew how to positively motivate employees through kindness and love, and some managers motivated through fear and positional authority. I observed that when employees were motivated through fear and positional authority, there was an initial quick change in behavior, but that the change did not last long term, and that over time the employees would do little things to get back at the manager and the business. I also noticed that employees did not last long under managers of this sort. These managers seemed to be always hiring and having to train new employees. If their goal was a high employee turnover ratio, they were nailing it, let me tell you!

I personally went from being the top salesperson in the division to the bottom of the rankings depending on the leadership style of my managers. There were times I felt empowered and in control of my destiny, and times in which I felt discouraged and stuck in a worker's prison of sorts. I continued to marvel at how my performance, and the performance of my subordinates fluctuated based on the management style of our direct supervisors. I do not think that it was a coincidence that I had such diversity in the leadership styles of my managers over this period.

Because of these polarizing management and employee situations, I found myself researching various leadership styles and their effects on employee happiness, employee productivity, and employee turnover. My goal was to find a leadership style that helped remedy the negative effects that can result from an authoritative leader. And guess what? I found the leadership style of servant leadership! And guess what? The research substantiated the idea that employees of servant leaders are some of the happiest employees in the workforce. And not only that!... The employees of servant leaders are more productive because of their lower distress rates at work! Wow!!...I thought!!! What about the turnover rates?... Again, the data substantiated the idea that employees of servant leaders or in organizations that utilize servant leadership principles have reduced turnover rates. Hold on... Shut the front door and ring the bell because I think we have found it!!!

I learned that Servant Leaders have a unique ability to create a work environment that minimizes employee stress, allowing the employee to have a clear mind, which then leads to increased productivity, increased team cohesiveness, and increased employee happiness.

This whole situation was amazing! It was like I was living in a leadership petri dish, collecting real-time data while I was studying various leadership styles. It was then that I needed to choose a topic for my doctoral dissertation. How interesting? I had just been shown a real-world business problem to study and had found a leadership style that is a potential remedy to the problem. Wow! If this was not some sort of divine intervention, I don't know what it would be! My failure in the investment world which barred me from working in the industry opened a new door of a doctoral program studying servant leadership! Out of some of the darkest parts of my life have come some of the greatest miracles and divine direction. The path forward had come together!

I then wrote my dissertation on the role of love in servant leadership. I also decided to make my life work trying to become the best servant leader that I could be. It was no longer about money for me. It was about doing the right thing for the right reason. Loving employees to a higher level of performance and happiness. A greater purpose for leadership had emerged in my life, burying alive my worldly pursuits.

Coming full circle... You know the nonprofit organization thrift store that I donated all my finance books to? Well, my career is now working for them as a Job Coach, and it is my dream job as a servant leader. I love the associates that I work with daily, and I am grateful to be able to have the privilege of working with them. They are a light to me! Anyways, the rest is history... I have been a student of servant leadership ever since. Am I good at being a servant leader? Absolutely not! Are there some days in which I don't even resemble a servant leader? All the time! As with every other endeavor I start... I constantly fall on my face! Every day is a battle! This is why I sometimes wear combat boots to work (true story). The greatest task that anyone can take in this life, and for the rest of eternity, is to become more like our perfect example of leadership

Jesus Christ.

Chapter Two

Day One

SERVANT LEADERSHIP FLYOVER
FLIPPING THE ORGANIZATIONAL CHART
ACTION STEP: ABOUT DOING GOOD

Congratulations! You have made it through my long-winded introduction! If you can get through that you can get through anything! I believe in you! Just showing up is 90% of the effort and you have shown up!... Ok, let's get to work! Welcome to day one of the three-day servant leadership training workshop. Put on your flying goggles because we are going to do a 20,000-foot view flyover of what servant leadership is all about. (Insert pretend take off here) You are welcome to make plane takeoff noises if you would like... Brbrbrbrbrbrbrb! Ya you got it! Brbrbrbrbrbrbrbrbrbr! Ha Ha... wasn't that fun! Hey, seeing it in your mind is the first step of any journey!

Servant Leadership

Now that we are super high up in the sky let's see what servant leadership is! First off, this may be obvious, but it is a leadership style that is patterned after the life of Jesus Christ! Probably not breaking new ground there! However, I would like to share three scriptures that give us a great baseline to start with. Roll the curtains please!... In the tenth chapter of Acts we find the following verses!

42 But Jesus called them to him, and saith unto them, **Ye know that they which are accounted to rule over the Gentiles exercise lordship**

over them; and their great ones exercise authority upon them.

43 **But so shall it not be among you**: but **whosoever will be great among you, shall be your minister**:

44 And **whosoever of you will be the chiefest, shall be servant of all**. Mark 10: 42-44

Jesus taught his Apostles a very important leadership lesson. First, he told them what kind of leader they were not to be. They were not to exercise lordship or authority over others as others have done. Second, he told them in two sentences what type of leader they were to be. If they were to be great, they were to be a minister... and those who will be the chiefest shall be the servant of all. And there you have it! Stop your reading, close the book, full stop, let's go home! I am not even going to write the rest of the book.

So that is as simple as you get. If you are to be

a great leader, you are to be a minister and the greatest servant. The statement seems to fit in the same category as the first shall be last and the last shall be first.

The servant leader stands apart from others, flips the authoritative leadership model upside down, and stands as a beacon of light, in what can be a dark business world. The servant leader knows that if he or she is to be the greatest leader, they must be the greatest servant and minister to others.

Flipping the Organizational Chart

Are you ready to do some more flipping? Flip ya you are! I heard you! I am a good listener like a servant leader should be! Ok, so this is going to be simple! Servant leadership has a different view regarding the organizational chart. All you need to do is take your organizational chart and flip it upside down. Ok, have you done it? It should now look like an inverted triangle with the leader of your organization at the bottom. He is the servant of all the organization that is now above him. Whoever is above you on the, now flipped, organizational chart is who you have a responsibility to serve and ensure their success.

So, this is the theory behind the flip. When a

servant leader moves up the organizational ladder, essentially, he or she is increasing the number of individuals within the organization that he or she is to serve. He who is greatest is the servant of all! Your service-load is increased as you are promoted within the organization. Your stewardship is increased.

So, who do the front-line associates serve if there is no one above them in the now flipped chart? Great question! Keep them coming! We can learn this servant leadership as a team... and remember there is no me in team... huh... ya there is... that's not the saying!... oh well... Shout out to one of my supervisors for that joke!

Back to the question... so the front-line associates are to serve the customers. In fact, the whole organization is responsible for serving customers because they are above everyone in the new organizational chart! Wow, a servant leader organization has an army of employees and staff that all serve the customers! Talk about some 5 star google reviews for customer service! I want to shop there!

Action Step:
About Doing Good

Congratulations you have made it through your first day of servant leadership training! So far, we have done a lot of flipping. Not going to lie... servant leadership flips the whole business world upside down. These new servant leadership prescription lenses may take some time to get used to... but don't worry you will be seeing great vistas in the distance as you approach your leadership with greater purpose.

So, each lesson is going to have an action step that is attached to it. Don't worry, trust me...I am a doctor!... lol... So, this is my leadership prescription for the next week... and hopefully the rest of your life... Did I say that last bit our loud? You bet I did!... but let's just focus on one week!... Just easing the tension!!

In Acts 10:38 we learn that Jesus went about doing good. This is what I would like you to focus on for the next week, and if you're lucky... the rest of your life! Crud! did I say it again... Wherever you go in the organization I want you to go about doing good. See this guy in the picture on the cover? He is a stud if I have ever seen one! Be like him!

A breadbasket under one arm (ready to minister) and business plans in the other (ready to get the work done). And no... those are not vulture's circling, ready to eat alive the servant leader!... lol. He is ready to minister and serve! He is ready to go about doing good! So that is your assignment! You can do it!

As you go about doing good at work… as you lift the hands which hang down, as you strengthen the feeble knees, as you go about your business… I promise that you will find greater purpose, increased happiness, and fulfillment in the workplace. And, as a side benefit… your coworkers and employees may reduce or stop talking bad about you behind your back… There is always a silver lining! I had to throw that in there! It was a joke! I think Dr. Dust crossed the line on that one! Hey, this is my book, keep your thoughts out of it! ☐Relax… take a deep breath… it's ok, you are a new you now. You are going about doing good… focusing on the positive +++++++++++++++++.

Bonus Story:

One of the many tangents (He sees squirrels, and they are everywhere)

Ok, so let's take a little time out, because this is the very spot where I finished my second full day of typing and I have a little story for you. Welcome to Dr. Dustin's story time!! So, I spent two full days, morning to night at the library, sprinkled with hot tub visits throughout of course! The hot tub visits are critical! Could not have accomplished much without them! I actually want to write a book dedicated just to how amazing hot tubs are! I could tell you some hilariously funny hot-tub stories!

Anyway... reel it in Dustin! My tangents are like the *Inception* movie... lots of layers... tangents within tangents. Hold on for this wild action thriller! So anyway, I had woken up on the third day in a sort of delirium but was determined to achieve my goal of writing a publishing this book in three days! I went to my wonderful Wife and said... Well... I will be home when my book is done! She said with a twinkle in her eyes... "So, are you not coming home for a few weeks?"... She then said, "you know... why do you push yourself so hard with these things? The kids are home from school today and will be home alone while I am at work. They have hardly any snacks to eat, and the car needs an oil change before our daughter takes it on her trip tomorrow."

So, there I was... insert long pause here... I had a choice to make... I could either set out to finish my three-day goal of writing a book about leading like Jesus, or I could be like Jesus and spend time with my kids, buy them snacks, and get the oil changed in the car. Sooooooooo... wait for it......................... I finished the book!!! ☐

I sure hope you didn't believe me! With emotions welling up in my eyes, I can tell you that spending time with my kids that day was one of the most cherished days that I have had lately! We got gas-station snacks not only once but twice, watched multiple movies, and went to our favorite swimming park! At the end of the day, I found myself thanking Heavenly Father for such a wonderful day with amazing kids! The oil change even got done! Hey, academic pursuits are important, but sometimes getting your oil changed is more importanter...lol... lube long and prosper!!

Let's come full circle because I don't think that it was an accident that this situation was placed in my path. There will be situations that come up in the workplace where you are going to have to choose between a to-do list that is growing by the minute, and an opportunity to minister to one of your associates in need. This reminds me of a quote by Thomas S. Monson that my daughter uses against me. "Never let a problem to be solved become more important than a person to be loved." Remember if you are to be a great leader... as Jesus said... you are to be a minister, and a servant. Boy... Dustin sure uses those three little dot things in this book a lot!!! I don't even think he is using them right!!! Hey! Keep your thoughts out of my book again!... !... !... !...

Anyway...lol... So, you know the quote... "Do what is right and let the consequences follow." So did I hit my goal of writing and publishing this book in three days?... Absolutely not! That was eight years ago!!!!... Remember, I am the fall on my face man, and why would I change that! No... just kidding... I am going to try and keep it to a solid four or five days to knock this puppy out!

Great luck on going about doing good this week!

Chapter Three

Day Two

LESSONS FROM THE HOT TUB
JESUS IS THE GREATEST LEADER BECAUSE...
SETTING THE BUSINESS ENVIRONMENT
ACTION STEP: EASING THE BURDENS OF THOSE WHO
REPORT TO YOU

Welcome back my servant leaders who have

been going about doing good! You are amazing!

Thanks for changing the business world one good act

at a time, one soul at a time.

Ok let's get right to the hot tub! Let me tell you something about me. I have always had a hard time holding still. I seem to always need to be doing something, accomplishing something. If I am not moving, I seem to sink into a type of sadness or depression. Whenever I would go to my grandfather or Father for advice when I was down or discouraged, they would say... "busy hands are happy hands." They were both masons by trade, so they made a living with their busy hands. After receiving this advice, I have made a conscious effort to remain busy in most areas of my life. If your body is moving and accomplishing things it knows that it is alive... and you feel invigorated. That is just the way I see it. Sitting at a desk at work drives me bat crud crazy! Keeping it family friendly for you!

My Wife would tell you that I am either moving or sleeping. It drives her crazy that I don't have a middle ground...except... wait for it.. except for when it comes to the hot tub... the heaven-sent hot tub!! You see, this is the one place where I can relax and be still, and this is amazing. I feel a deep sense of sympathy for our pioneer

forefathers because they have not experienced this bliss. And can I say how stunningly similar this image is to what I look like! It feels like I am looking in the

mirror!   Right Zoe? (my wife)...   Zoe?... Hello?...
Zoe?...

I go to this wondrous magical place as often as occasion will permit... so between four and six times per week. I have even had days where I go two or three times in a day. I use the hot tub to relax, stretch, pray, and dial back to zero. I can pray there because no one thinks it is weird for someone to be relaxing with their eyes closed in the hot tub. And no, I do not own any stock in a hot tub company... no ethical dilemmas on this one! I can even cry in the hot tub, and no one is the wiser, because of already having beads of sweat all over my face! If you hit the tub early in the morning or late at night, you will likely have the place to yourself.   Also, not to mention the side benefit of burning about one hundred forty calories per hour sitting in a 104 degree hot tub! Ha! Don't believe me? Look it up! It is the same as taking a 30-minute walk! This is a perfect example of a win-win situation! Just this one piece of information may transform your life! You are welcome!

So, this morning, I went to the gym to work out and sit in the hot tub. I was praying about what the second day of servant leadership training should be when one of my friends came and sat next to me in the hot tub. This man is someone who I admire and respect and gave one of my favorite speeches on the topic I am writing about. He has also successfully run and led many successful organizations. He is amazing! The spirit whispered to me... "One of my servants is next to you... why don't you ask him?" Of course, being me, I blew it off, not wanting to bother him. After about fifteen minutes I again received an urge to tell him about my project and ask him for his advice. This time I listened, told him about my project, and asked him for advice. So, I just sat there and did a double soak.

I soaked in his advice, and soaked in the heat from the hot tub... while burning calories. Talk about a triple win! I am so glad that I spoke to him. It was an answer to my prayer.

He said that to be a great leader you need to be a great follower. The greatest leaders are the greatest followers, they are humble. Jesus was the greatest leader because he was the greatest follower of His Father's will and plan. He presented himself to be our Savior but did not come into it saying or thinking that he had all the answers. He was a humble follower of His Father and humbly went about doing His Fathers work. So here we go again servant leadership flipping the business leadership perspective upside down. Let's say this again... Jesus is the greatest leader because he is the greatest follower, he is humble.

Talk About Changing the Environment

Who is ready to plant some trees! Ya, come-on let's start hugging those trees! It feels good to hug trees! What you have never done it! Don't diss it until you try it! I bet it hugs you back! Lol... Let's change the environment!

Not that environment Dustin! The work environment. Why does the work environment matter? Ok, so let's lay out a few figures. So, if the average person works 35 hours per week, this will total to around 1,800 hours per year, and somewhere around 90,000 hours by retirement. This is roughly 1/3 of a person's working life. As a leader you get the opportunity to create a flipping amazing work environment for those you lead that will take up a significant portion of their life! What a responsibility!

The leader has a profound impact on the work environment. How you act, your demeanor, how you behave, and work as a leader is contagious. Not just a little contagious... a lot contagious. I mean if there was a deadly virus as contagious as this there would be no life on earth! I don't even think triple masking and 6-foot social distancing policy would stop this leadership virus from spreading! Let's spread the leadership contagion of a great attitude and a positive work environment!

Ok, servant leader, you have the amazing responsibly to create a positive work environment for your employees. Jesus Christ is the creator of the world on which you are reading this book. Creation is profoundly important. The business environment you have stewardship for is your canvas, and you have the environmental paints at your disposal. Your mood matters to your team, the way you approach them matters, the way you help them matters, and the way you teach them matters.

Remember, becoming like the Savior in your leadership activities is a lifelong process, and so falling on your face, getting up, and recommitting to being better is a process that you will have go through repeatedly. Remember, the words: I am sorry, please forgive me, and I will do better next time go a long way... especially as a leader! And to quote one of my favorite managers... "change is a process... not an event." You can do it! Just like when I am eating a steak as big as my face... I say "I am going to eat this whole plate because I am not a quitter... I am a finisher... even if I get gout!"

Action Step: Easing the Burdens of your Direct Reports

Ok action steppers... are you excited for this week's edition of (insert loud radio voice) ACTION IN SERVANT LEADERSHIP!!! There are two amazing scriptures in Galatians 6 that I would like to share. Paul the Apostle in writing to the Galatians stated:

2 Bear ye one another's burdens, and so fulfil the law of Christ.

9 And let us not be weary in well doing:

This week the action step is to look for, find, and implement ways to help ease the burdens of your team. This could be looking for ways to make their processes smoother and more efficient for them, it could be you working with them side by side to help them achieve organizational goals, it could be anything that would help alleviate a small portion of the weight they feel. I can promise you that the employees will appreciate your work on their behalf.

Servant leaders are all about serving the needs of those around them, even when it does not benefit them directly. They are not weary in well doing. Servant leadership is difficult to implement from the office, so yes... push your chair under your desk, roll up your sleeves, and start alleviating the burdens of others through your selfless service. This has nothing to do with positioning yourself for a promotion. It has everything to do with doing the right thing for the right reason for the benefit of others.

Your employees will enjoy a healthy work environment, have increased productivity because of less distress, and your employee turnover rate will decrease magnificently.

Traditionally, the employees are seen to be servants of the manager or leader. This is another instance where servant leadership flips the traditional upside down! Get used to it my brother or sister in Christ. In servant leadership, the leader serves the employee's needs first and helps them be as successful as possible.

I can tell you that you will feel the warm fuzzies while completing this week's action step! Just like watching a Hallmark movie during Christmas! It just feels good to serve others, and to alleviate burdens. So where do you think those good feelings come from?... Good luck alleviating the burdens of those who report to you!

Chapter Four

Day Three

ALL HE'S EVER BEEN IS KIND
THE FEEDBACK OF CORRECTION
ACTION STEP: ARMED WITH EXAMPLE

Wow! Where has the time gone! We are on
the last day of servant leadership training! I have
been praying about what topic should be on the

docket for today, and I just can't seem to get the phrase out of my head..." All He's ever been is kind." This is a line from one of my favorite Christian songs titled *Kind* by *Cory Asbury*. Kindness is one of the attributes of Christ. I remember learning about kindness in business relations back when I was taking a kindness course for my MBA... HaHa... not... The aim of this book has been to teach a subject of leadership and business management that is not learned through attending higher education. It is usually leaned through a lifetime of experiences, some of which can be very painful. I had a wise manager once tell me the following story...

"While I was attending university, I had a professor who brought a cart stacked with tall stacks of self-improvement and management books. The professor told us that he had read every book in the cart. He then said that he was going to save all the students the time of having to read all the stacks of books and sum up the lesson in just two words. He then said the two words are *be kind*."

My father-in-law was arguably one of the best job coaches of his time. I learned many life lessons from him during his job-coaching career. There is one line that he stated repeatedly...

"You don't know what difficult challenges each person is facing in their life... therefore, it is important that we are more kind than necessary."

Looking back on my life I can safely say that I have never regretted being kind. On the flip side, some of the most painful experiences I have experienced have come from times when I was lacking in kindness. Servant Leaders are Kind.

The Feedback of Correction

This section is going to be super short, but it is going to have a one-line quote that will stick with you for a lifetime. Once again, I bring my father-in-law back into the picture. He told me multiple times the following quote:

"See everything, praise a lot, correct a little."

The servant leader sees everything because he or she is not in the office. Heaps and heaps of praise are what typically falls from the lips of the servant leader. Whenever possible, building on the strengths of employees is focused on. When correction and or accountability does need to be made, it is done with love, and is not done in front of others. Correction is also conveyed with the leader's metaphorical arm wrapped around the employee. (don't want any harassment claims here)... Love leads the day when correction is made. I am sad to say that I have not always utilized love when correcting or holding others accountable. Think back to when you had to be corrected by a superior. How did you feel the rest of the day? It takes more skill and care to correct others with love, but the outcome is much better. This is another lesson that I have painfully learned and still fail at daily!

My father-in-law would often say that if one of his managers approached him with love when a change needed to be made, he would go to heaven and back to make the correction. If he was approached without love, using positional authority, he would dig in his heals and resist change and fight against it. It is just human behavior.

You don't want to be a seagull leader... just flying around pooping on everyone... pointing out their short comings. I don't have to cite a study to tell you that you can accomplish more by focusing on and building on the strengths of others, rather than pointing out weaknesses. This is not to say that servant leaders do not point out things that need to change. They do, but it is done one on one, not in front of coworkers, and is done in a positive and motivating way... surrounded with love.

Action Step: Armed With Example

Ok, I am going to be super honest. I am basically at the end of my third day of typing this book. It is currently 3 AM in the morning. I think I am experiencing a small dose of delirium. I have been drinking Diet Mt. Dew and eating my feelings all night. I am not sure if an hour sitting in the hot tub will make up for the massive number of calories I have consumed. I can feel my love handles becoming muffin tops... lol... Hmm... I could go for a muffin right now! Chocolate with chocolate chunks please! I wonder if 7-Eleven is open? of course it is! A chili cheese dog sounds amazing as well!

Ok, I am motivated! Let's do the last action step!

Servant leaders are do as I do type of people, and they lead through their example. When you are consistently living up to the same standards that you hold others accountable for you are armed with the power of example. The power of example goes a long way! Now, can you hold others accountable for being late while you are consistently late? Of course you can! This is called being a hypocrite, and your employees will be throwing you under a bus faster than I can eat a muffin and a chili cheese dog after finishing this tonight. But!... when you are armed with the power of example, you are not only providing a great example for your employees to follow... you can speak your mind your voice and your will when motivating, teaching, and training employees. Jesus, in his concluding remarks in the sermon on the mount, stated the following:

3 And why beholdest thou the mote that is in thy brother's eye, but considerest not the

beam that is in thine own eye?

4 Or how wilt thou say to thy brother, Let me pull out the mote out of thine eye; and, behold, a beam is in thine own eye?

5 Thou hypocrite, first cast out the beam out of thine own eye; and then shalt thou see clearly to cast out the mote out of thy brother's eye (Matthew 7: 3-5).

This is your action step. I want you to cast the beam out of your own eye by being a great example for your employees to follow this week, and ... and... you should know this by now... for the rest of your life. You live by the standards you hold your employees to! You can do it! I know that your example will help inspire other leaders to do the same, will set a great example for your employees to follow, and will arm you with the power of example. Good luck this week!

Conclusion

So, all I can say is that this has been real and fun, but not real fun... Just Kidding... I hope that it has been real and fun for you. Thank you for taking the initiative of reading *The 3 Day Servant Leader*. I really do hope it has helped you in some way. Servant leadership happens at the corner of love and accountability, and results in employees being happy and healthy. (I hope I don't get legal action for stealing that line...lol).

Now, is there a lot more involved when it comes to servant leadership? Yes, you can go very deep into this subject. However, I once had an instructor who had two students hold a string that stretched across the room. He then called another student up and had this student use their finger to lift the string upward at one point along the string. The instructor then pointed out that even though upward movement was applied to only one part of the string, it affected lifted both sides of the string as well. It is like the saying a rising tide lifts all the ships.

Becoming amazing at just the few principles taught in this book will raise the tide and lift all your metaphorical ships. It will positively lift both sides of the string. It will spill into, affect, and improve all aspects of your life.

Final Action Step

Now, I am going to take this book a step further than the business world. My final action step to you is to let servant leadership principles be infused into who you are as an individual. Servant leadership is not an only at work leadership theory. It is a who you are striving to be as a person all the time leadership theory.

I want you to go about doing good in all aspects of your life. I want you to lift the burdens of your family for the rest of your life. I want you to be an example to your family for the rest of your life. I want you to correct and give advice to the ones you love with love. I want you to see your whole life as an opportunity to lead as the Savior would.

It is only in following our Savior Jesus Christ and emulating him in all aspects of our life that we can truly become more like Him. I have seen miracles happen through servant leadership. I have seen lives changed, marriages strengthened, friendships renewed, businesses revitalized, and commitment to Christ strengthened.

I wish you all the luck in the World as you change the business world and your own world through servant leadership principles. Go ahead servant leader! Oh, and yes, I ended up finishing this book in a 3 day period... Just not 3 consecutive days. Treat yourself. Go and get you a Chocolate Muffin! You have done great! The End!

Notes

Notes

Notes

Notes